Shiv Celebration

Being Good

We will be with family.

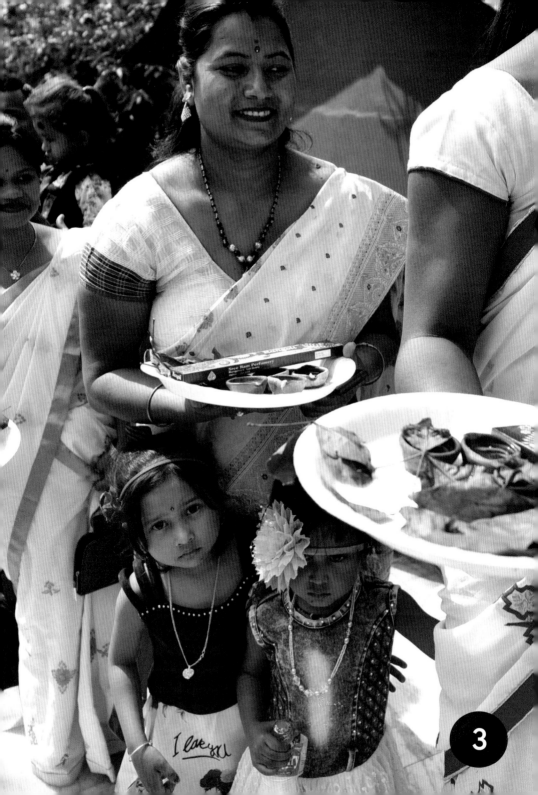

We will eat special food.

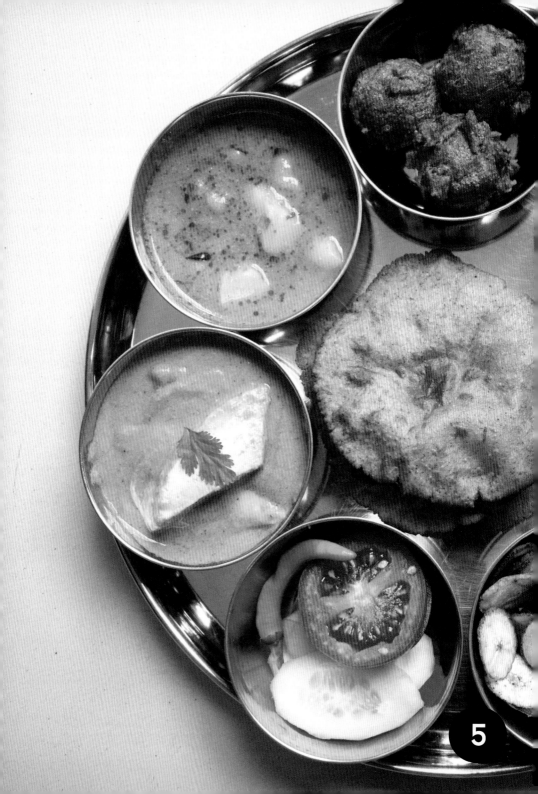

5

We will see the flowers.

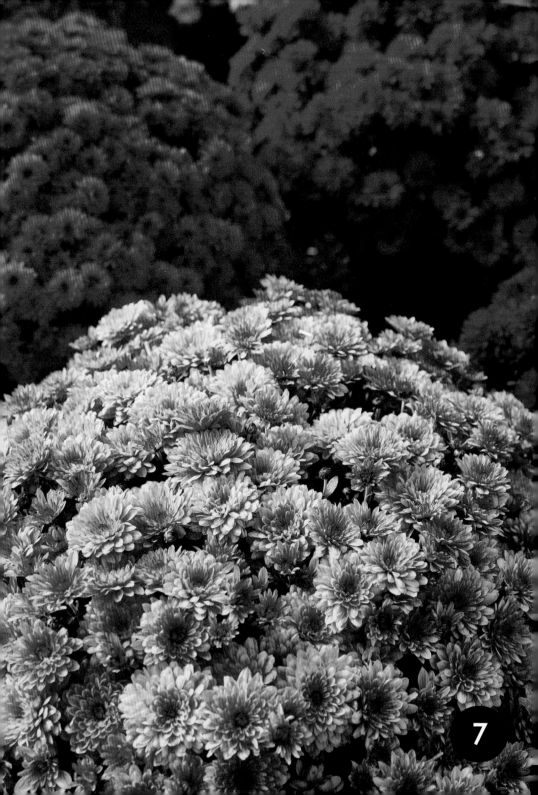

We will swim in the river.

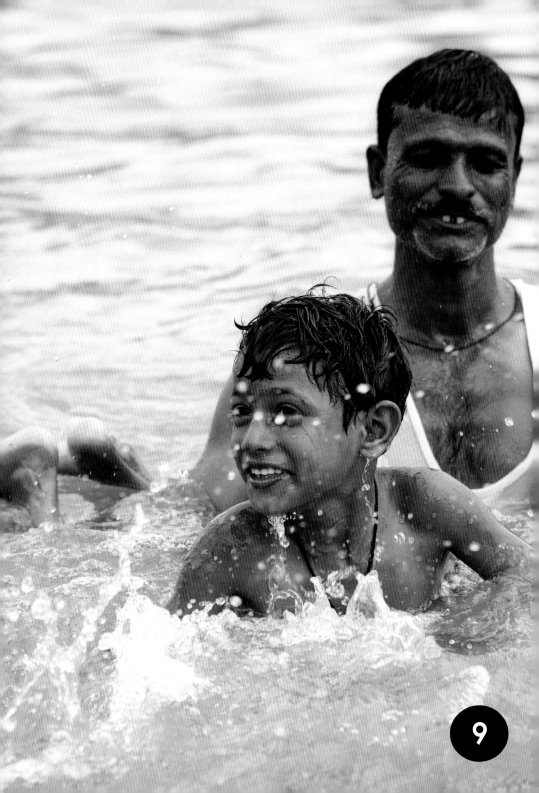

We will go to the parade.

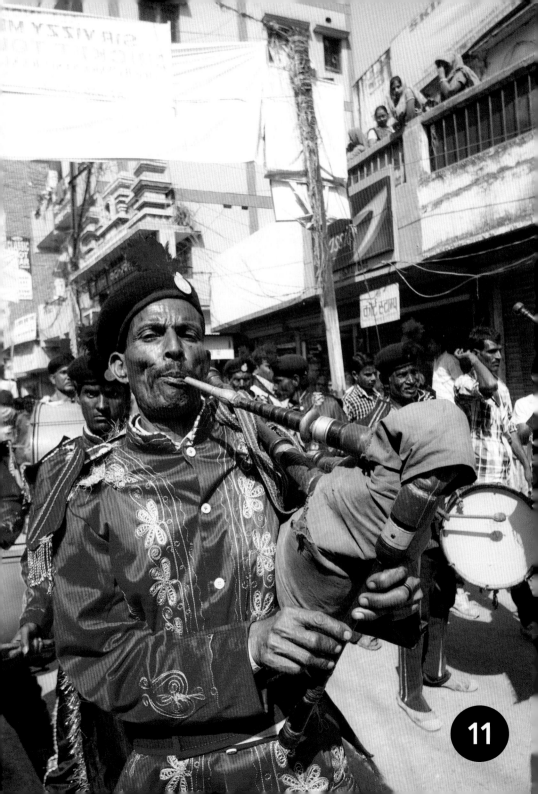

11

We will go to the temple.

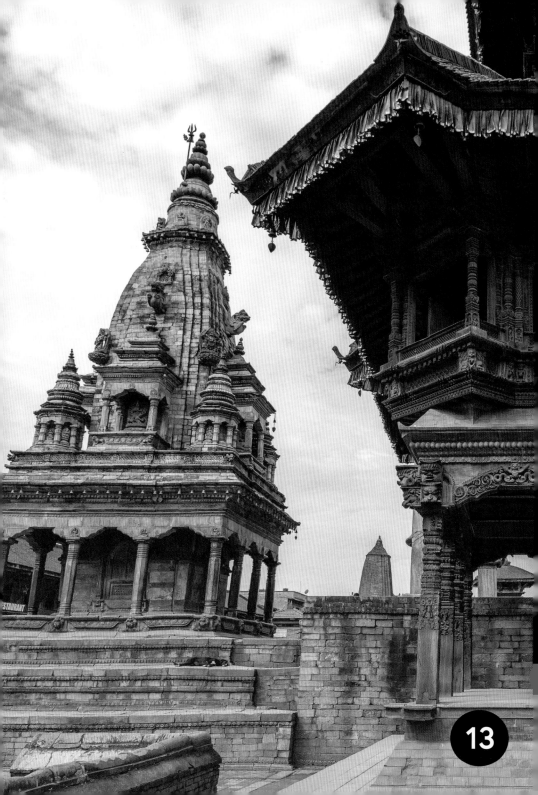

13

We will sit like this.

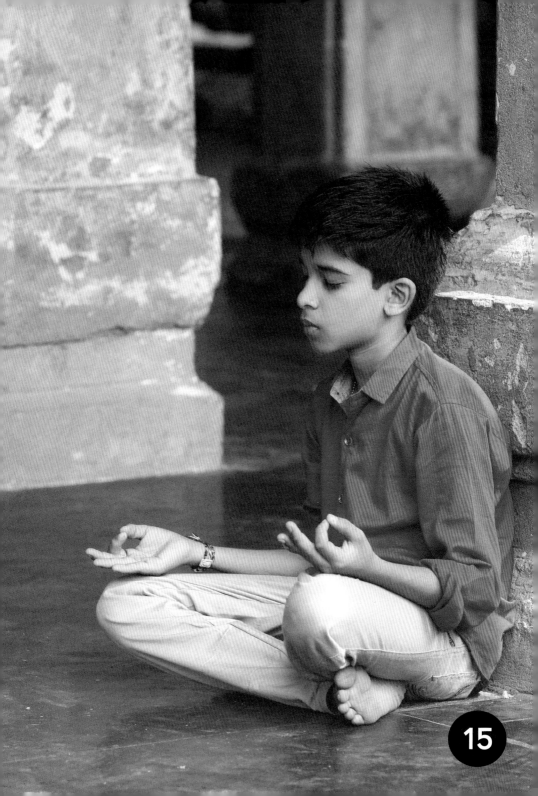

15

We will hear the bells.

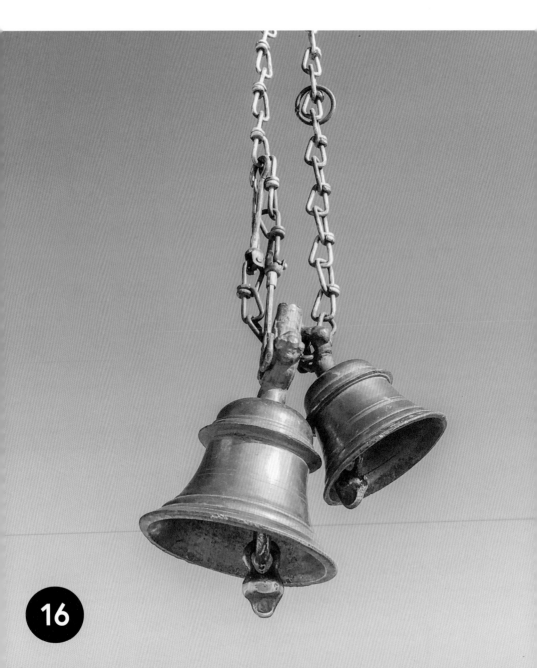